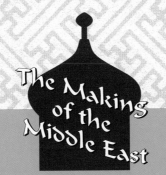

The Making of the Middle East

The Ottoman and Qajar Empires in the Age of Reform

The Ottoman and Qajar Empires in the Age of Reform

Hal Marcovitz

Mason Crest Publishers
Philadelphia

Frontispiece: Ornate tilework from the Persian mosque at Isfahan.

Produced by OTTN Publishing, Stockton, N.J.

Mason Crest Publishers
370 Reed Road
Broomall, PA 19008
www.masoncrest.com

First printing

1 3 5 7 9 8 6 4 2

Library of Congress Cataloging-in-Publication Data

Marcovitz, Hal.
   The Ottoman and Qajar empires in the age of reform / Hal Marcovitz.
      p. cm. — (The making of the Middle East)
   Includes bibliographical references and index.
   ISBN-13: 978-1-4222-0167-1
   ISBN-10: 1-4222-0167-8
   1. Turkey—History—Tanzimat, 1839-1876—Juvenile literature. 2. Turkey—History—1878-1909—
Juvenile literature. 3. Turkey—History—Mehmed V, 1909-1918—Juvenile literature. 4. Iran—History—
Qajar dynasty, 1794-1925—Juvenile literature. I. Title.
   DR565.M37 2007
   955'.04—dc22
                        2007029042

Table of Contents

Introduction:
The Importance of the Middle East

The region known as the Middle East has a significant impact on world affairs. The countries of the greater Middle East—the Arab states of the Arabian Peninsula, Eastern Mediterranean, and North Africa, along with Israel, Turkey, Iran, and Afghanistan—possess a large portion of the world's oil, a valuable commodity that is the key to modern economies. The region also gave birth to three of the world's major faiths: Judaism, Christianity, and Islam.

In recent years it has become obvious that events in the Middle East affect the security and prosperity of the rest of the world. But although such issues as the wars in Iraq and Afghanistan, the floundering Israeli-Palestinian peace process, and the struggles within countries like Lebanon and Sudan are often in the news, few Americans understand the turbulent history of this region.

Human civilization in the Middle East dates back more than 8,000 years, but in many cases the modern conflicts and issues in the region can be attributed to events and decisions made during the past 150 years. In particular, after World War I ended in 1918, the victorious Allies—especially France and Great Britain—redrew the map of the Middle East, creating a number of new countries, such as Iraq, Jordan, and Syria. Other states, such as Egypt and Iran, were dominated by foreign powers until after the Second World War. Many of the Middle Eastern countries did not become independent until the 1960s or 1970s. Political and economic developments in the Middle Eastern states over the past four decades have shaped the region's direction and led to today's headlines.

The purpose of the MAKING OF THE MIDDLE EAST series is to nurture a better understanding of this critical region, by providing the basic history along

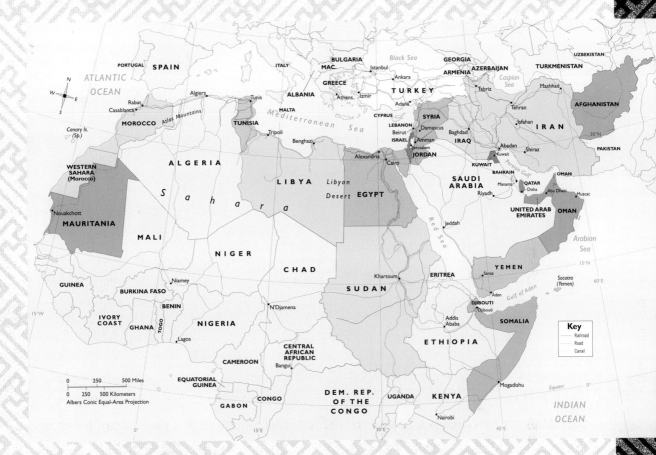

with explanation and analysis of trends, decisions, and events. Books will examine important movements in the Middle East, such as the development of nationalism in the 1880s and the rise of Islamism from the 1970s to the present day.

The 10 volumes in the MAKING OF THE MIDDLE EAST series are written in clear, accessible prose and are illustrated with numerous historical photos and maps. The series should spark students' interest, providing future decision-makers with a solid foundation for understanding an area of critical importance to the United States and the world.

By the 19th century, the once mighty Persian and Ottoman empires had fallen into a state of decline. (Opposite) A mosque in Tehran, which became the capital of Persia when the first Qajar ruler, Agha Mohammad Khan, came to power in 1795. (Right) The sun sets over Istanbul, the Ottoman capital.

1 A Tale of Two Empires

*T*he 19th century was a time of tremendous change for two major empires in the greater Middle East, the Persian Empire and the Ottoman Empire. For many years the rulers of these empires had reigned with unquestioned authority over large territories populated with subjects who had diverse cultural and ethnic backgrounds. However, growing internal and external pressure during the 1800s eventually forced leaders of both empires to implement reforms in order to maintain their hold on power.

The Ottoman Empire

The Ottoman Empire was established in 1299 by Osman I, a Turkish-speaking Muslim who united a group of tiny states in what was known as Asia Minor, or the Anatolian Peninsula. This region of 780,000 square miles (2,020,191 square kilometers) straddles eastern Europe and the Middle East, and has great strategic importance. European merchants traveling to Asia along the Silk Road—an ancient network of trade routes that connected communities in the Mediterranean region to China—had to pass through Anatolia, where they paid steep taxes to the Ottoman rulers.

By the 16th century, the empire was a major world power, controlling some 30 million subjects dispersed over a vast expanse of territory that spanned three continents and stretched from the Danube to the Nile. Ottoman lands included a quarter of Europe, parts of North Africa, and the Middle East, including most of the great cities of Islam—Damascus, Mecca, Medina, Jerusalem, Cairo, Tunis, and Baghdad.

The center of the Empire was Istanbul (formerly the Roman capital of Constantinople). From the ancient city, Ottoman sultans ruled over a multi-ethnic population of Turks, Arabs, Kurds, Armenians, Slavs, and others. The empire's subjects included Muslims, Christians, and Jews, and the Muslim sultans ruled not only as political leaders but also as supreme military, judicial, social, and religious leaders.

By the end of the 18th century, however, the empire had started to collapse after suffering a series of setbacks: military defeats, failed attempts at modernization, internal degeneration, and external pressures from foreign powers. Across Europe, a sense of nationalism would soon start driving revolutionary movements in Greece, the Balkans, and elsewhere within the Ottoman Empire. The Ottoman rulers found themselves standing at the crossroads of history after nearly five centuries as the world's largest independent Islamic empire.

The Qajar Dynasty of Persia

In neighboring Persia (present-day Iran), a new ruling regime, the Qajar dynasty, took power in 1794. The Qajar shahs presided over a much smaller and weaker empire than the Ottoman sultans—Persia was slightly larger in area than the state of Alaska, with a population of about 6 million in 1800. But ancient Persia (a word stemming from the name Pars) had always been a place of strategic importance in the world because of its location. The land that is now called Iran sits at the crossroads of Europe, Asia, and India, and like the Anatolian Peninsula is on the Silk Road.

The first Qajar ruler, Agha Mohammad Khan Qajar, emerged in 1794 following a 15-year civil war that pitted the country's many diverse tribes against one another. Agha Mohammad used ruthless tactics to wipe out his main adversary, the Zand tribe, and unite Persia under his rule in 1796. Although he only ruled for a short time—the year after he crowned himself shah, Agha Mohammad was assassinated by his servants—he succeeded in winning back lands that Persia had previously lost to Russia, namely territories in Georgia and the Caucasus, and he established the Persian capital at Tehran.

Agha Mohammad's successors lacked his ruthlessness, as well as his success on the battlefield. Over the next century, the Qajar shahs would

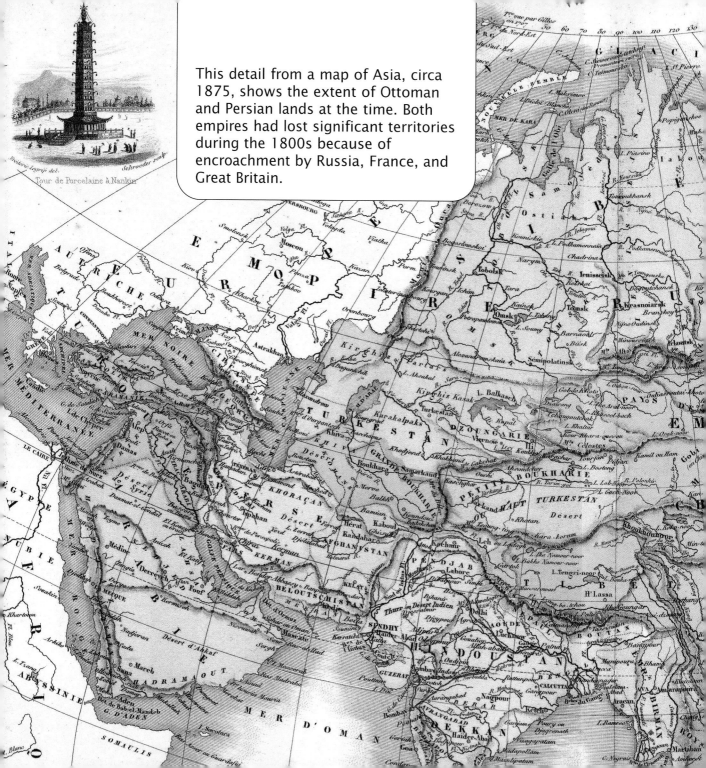

This detail from a map of Asia, circa 1875, shows the extent of Ottoman and Persian lands at the time. Both empires had lost significant territories during the 1800s because of encroachment by Russia, France, and Great Britain.

gradually embrace Western trends in commerce, education, culture, and fashion. However, the influence of foreign powers would also pose a serious threat to Persia's independence. In particular, Great Britain and the Russian Empire became involved in Persian affairs to protect their own interests in the Middle East and Central Asia during the 19th and early 20th centuries.

(Opposite) The French ruler Napoleon greets a Persian ambassador, 1807. Under Napoleon the French had conquered the Ottoman province of Egypt a decade earlier. (Right) Britain was interested in the Middle East in order to protect its valuable colony in India. The famous Taj Mahal is pictured.

2 Empires Under Pressure

As the Ottomans presided over a crumbling empire and the Qajars labored to modernize their kingdom, three world powers set their sights on their territory. Throughout the 19th century Great Britain, France, and the Russian Empire attempted to exert economic, military, and political influence over the Middle East, Africa, and Europe by acquiring new lands containing valuable raw materials, and developing profitable markets and trade routes.

But although each of these European powers managed to gain territory from the Ottoman and Qajar empires, at other times they sided with the Turks and Persians to thwart the efforts of their rivals. The European powers were suspicious of one another's motives, and often willing to step in and act as a check against another power's ambitions.

Great Britain's Industrial Machine

By the early years of the 19th century, Great Britain had established itself as a military and industrial leader in the world. Britain maintained the largest and most powerful navy on Earth, and it also possessed the world's most modern weaponry and technology. Dramatic and rapid change had also taken root in Great Britain's economy, as the society changed from an agricultural fiefdom to an industrialized nation. England's rural citizens flocked to the cities to find factory jobs. Practically overnight, small villages such as Manchester, Birmingham, Sheffield, and Leeds became major industrial cities. Major improvements to the country's infrastructure, and a highly efficient system of government further contributed to Great Britain's rapid growth.

Britain's economic advancement depended largely on foreign trade. England's vast merchant fleet carried goods and raw materials throughout the British Empire, which by the 19th century stretched from Canada to Australia and included colonies in Africa, the Caribbean, South America, and Asia. The jewel of the crown was India, from which the British exported silk, cotton, tea, dyes, spices, and hundreds of other products. The British kept thousands of troops stationed in India, in part to oversee the empire's valuable resources but also to serve as a base for further expansion into Asia.

To protect its farflung network of overseas colonies, and to facilitate the international trade on which the empire was based, Great Britain developed a powerful navy.

Other nations eyed British India and hoped to share in the wealth. One of those nations was France. Like England, France would grow into an industrial power during the 19th century, as well as a center of European banking, arts, and culture. By the early 1800s France had come under the rule of Napoleon Bonaparte, who harbored ambitions to seize India from France's longtime rival.

The Battle over Egypt

In 1798 Napoleon, then an artillery officer, was placed in charge of 50,000 French soldiers and a fleet to ferry them to the Middle East with the eventual goal of invading India. On July 1 Napoleon and his men landed in the Mediterranean port city of Alexandria, Egypt.

Egypt had been part of the Ottoman Empire since 1517. However, the Ottoman force in Egypt was unable to stop Napoleon. The French army easily suppressed the defenders of Alexandria, and marched 150 miles to the Egyptian capital at Cairo. As Napoleon's men neared Cairo, they defeated poorly armed cavalry soldiers at what became known as the Battle of the Pyramids, on July 21, 1798. A day later, an emissary from the Ottoman ambassador in Cairo arrived in Napoleon's camp to deliver the formal surrender. On July 23 the French army marched into Cairo.

The French remained in Egypt for three years. During their occupation, they pushed farther into the Middle East, marching across the Sinai Desert to defeat a Turkish army at Jaffa in what is today Israel. But after moving even farther north, they were defeated by the Ottoman Turks at the city of Acre, thanks in part to provisions and ammunition supplied to the Ottoman soldiers by the British. Retreating from Acre, Napoleon realized he did not have enough soldiers to dominate the Middle East and threaten India. After retreating from Acre, he lamented, "I would have been master of the key to the Orient. I would have gone on to Constantinople."

In August 1799 the government in Paris recalled Napoleon to help defend the country from an expected attack by other European countries.

Early in 1801 a joint force of Ottoman and British soldiers surrounded Cairo. The French garrison defended the city for seven months but finally surrendered. The British occupied Egypt for a brief period, but in 1802, satisfied that the Middle East was now secure and that France no longer posed a threat to India, returned control to the Ottoman Turks.

In 1805 the Ottoman sultan appointed an Albanian military commander named Muhammad Ali governor of Egypt. He wielded the Egyptians into a powerful fighting force and remained in power for 44 years. He also grew bold and independent of the Ottoman rulers in Constantinople; in 1840, Sultan Abdulmecid I grudgingly granted Muhammad Ali's hereditary right to rule Egypt. His heirs would remain in power into the 20th century.

Napoleon, after taking power in France and proclaiming himself emperor, continued to harbor ambitions of seizing India from the British. He also believed his army capable of conquering the Ottoman Empire. However, threats to French power from elsewhere in the world kept him from realizing those dreams.

Although Muhammad Ali (1769–1849) was chosen by the sultan to serve as viceroy of Egypt, he eventually attempted to break the province away from the Ottoman Empire. After two wars, he won the right for his descendants to rule Egypt after his death.

Expansion of the Russian Empire

Another major power of the time was the enormous Russian Empire, which stretched from Europe to the Pacific Ocean. Because many Russian ports were choked with ice for much of the year, Russian leaders had long desired to expand the empire south and gain access to warm-water ports. The Ottoman Empire became a target for Russia because the sultans controlled the Bosporus, a strait that connected the Black Sea to the Mediterranean and therefore could be used to impede the progress of Russian ships. Great Britain and France also considered Russia a threat to their interests. The British in particular sought to keep Russia safely contained in the Black Sea and away from British India and its route to Egypt.

Russia was far less industrialized than either France or Great Britain, but it was no less of a power, due mostly to its sprawling territory and population of more than 25 million people. The influential French diplomat Charles Maurice de Talleyrand-Périgord concluded in 1816 that "France and Austria would be the strongest powers in Europe if, during the last century, another power [Russia] had not risen in the North." The diplomat described Russia's rapid expansion as "terrible" and predicted "that the numerous encroachments by which she has already signaled herself are but the prelude of still further conquests, which will end in swallowing up everything."

There was reason for Talleyrand-Périgord's dire prediction. Under the empress Catherine the Great, Russia had pushed its frontiers outward, often at the expense of the Ottoman Turks who twice lost wars to Catherine's armies in the late 1700s. After her death in 1796, Catherine was

A political cartoon from 1791 depicts Russian ruler Catherine the Great as a bear engaged in conflict with Britain, represented by King George III and his ministers. Throughout the 19th century both Britain and Russia were interested in gaining influence over Central Asia.

succeeded briefly by a son, Paul, who was assassinated by Russian nobles in 1801. Paul's successor, his son Alexander I, proved to be a much more capable tsar, ruling for 24 years. Alexander introduced a number of liberal reforms to his people. He established schools and universities, instructed the courts to treat all defendants fairly, encouraged the importation of foreign-published books, and sponsored many building projects in St. Petersburg, the capital city.

Like France, Russia had often cast an envious eye on India. In 1800, Tsar Paul had offered to strike an alliance with Napoleon to invade India; the French leader declined. Alexander's relations with Napoleon were far less cordial; their countries fought a bitter war in 1812 and 1813. Both sides hoped to gain military superiority on the European continent, which would allow an attack on British India. Napoleon's troops ventured far into Russia and burned Moscow, but the French army was eventually beaten back by Alexander's troops and the bitterly cold Russian winter.

The defeated French returned home to await their fate; for Napoleon, the loss meant exile. In 1815, when all the European powers convened at the Congress of Vienna to carve up France's former holdings, Russia took dominion over Poland, while England gained islands in the eastern Mediterranean. The British could now establish naval bases to protect India and its interests in the Middle East.

The Loss of Algeria and Greece

The Ottoman Empire was also involved with conflicts involving the British, French, and Russians. Several decades after winning Egypt back from France, the Turks would find themselves under siege from the French again. This time, the French challenged Ottoman authority in Algeria, on the coast of North Africa.

The Turks had assumed control of Algeria in 1518. They had arrived not as conquerors, but as defenders intent on protecting Algerian Muslims who had fallen under the occupation of Christians from Spain. After gaining control over the territory, the Ottoman Turks mostly stayed out of Algerian affairs, satisfied to simply collect taxes on the bountiful booty captured by Algerian pirates.

The 1814 Treaty of Paris, signed after Napoleon's defeat in Russia, had stripped France of territories that it had gained between 1795 and 1812. It also restored the Bourbon monarchy. Over the next decade the new French king, Charles X, labored to rebuild the country's standing among European powers. Eventually, the French resurrected their expansionist ambitions. In 1829, Charles's chief minister Jules Armand de Polignac began a policy of French colonization in Algeria, and the next year France annexed the territory. The Ottoman Turks left the fight to the Algerians, who were no match for the invading French army.

At around the same time, the Ottoman Empire was forced to grant independence to its Greek territories, which had begun fighting the Turkish regime in 1821. Many Europeans sympathized with the Greek rebellion, and Great Britain, France, and Russia provided military and financial assistance during the Greek War for Independence. In the 1832 Treaty of Constantinople, the Ottoman sultan officially recognized the modern state of Greece.

Soon, the Ottomans would face other problems. During the 1830s Russia began making bold incursions into the Balkans, attacking Ottoman forts and attempting to undermine imperial control. This was part of the tsars' dream of uniting all Slavic people under their rule. In Egypt, meanwhile, Muhammad Ali was seeking independence from the Ottoman Empire.

Trouble in the Caucasus Mountains

In Persia Fath Ali faced his own problems with encroachment by Europeans. The territory northwest of Persia, just below the Caucasus Mountains, had long been in dispute. In that region, the country of Georgia had been divided between Persian and Ottoman rule since the 16th century. But in 1783 the Russians under Catherine the Great invaded Georgia under the pretext of protecting its Christian population from Islamic rule. The real reason for Russia's invasion was to take advantage of Georgia's warm weather port cities on the Black Sea. In 1804 Fath Ali sent an army to regain Georgia. However, although the Persians put up a good fight—the war lasted until 1813—Fath Ali's soldiers were no match for the Russian army.

During the war Fath Ali was encouraged to keep fighting by the English, who

Fath Ali Shah (1771–1834), the second Qajar shah, was the nephew of Agha Mohammad Khan. During his rule, Persia lost two costly wars with Russia.

rightly feared that the Russians intended to push further into the Middle East and eventually to India. To keep the conflict going the British ferried munitions and supplies to Fath Ali's troops. However, in 1812 the Russians and English formed an alliance against Napoleon, so the Persians suddenly found themselves waging the war on their own.

In 1813 Fath Ali finally called a halt to the war with Russia. Under the terms of the treaty, Persia conceded Georgia to the Russian empire. Tsar Alexander also took control over the eastern portion of Armenia, Georgia's neighbor to the south. (The western portion was under Ottoman rule.)

The peace lasted just 13 years. From the beginning, the terms of the treaty remained in dispute; soon, the Persians complained that the Russians were extending their influence into neighboring Azerbaijan, which they contended had not been lost in the war. Muslim clerics also charged that Islamic citizens of Georgia were being mistreated by the Russian Christians. In 1826 Fath Ali sent his troops back into Georgia, this time with no support from Great Britain. Once again, the Iranians were no match for the superior firepower of the Russian army. The fighting lasted two years. This time, the terms of the surrender required Fath Ali to turn over Azerbaijan to the Russians.

(Opposite) During the long reign of Nasser al-Din, many western innovations were introduced into Persian life. (Right) It was in this building in Shiraz that a Persian merchant named Mirza Ali Mohammad declared that he was a prophet, taking the title Bab. The development of Babism threatened the stability of the Qajar regime.

3 Nasser al-Din and the Era of Reform

Iranians seethed over the two disastrous wars with Russia, but Fath Ali had no heart for more fighting. When he died in 1834 his empire was at peace, but his people remained in poverty. There was virtually no opportunity for education in Iran. The country's few factories manufactured little. Trade was carried out in busy street bazaars, but foreign goods were rare. Since the 16th century, Persia had maintained an uneasy peace with its western neighbor, the Ottoman Empire. Border clashes were common, and the Ottomans had all but cut off commerce to Persia.

Arriving in this environment was Fath Ali's successor, his grandson Mohammad Shah Qajar. The new shah was anxious to reestablish Persia as a power in the Middle East, and in 1837 he sent an army east into Afghanistan to attack the English-held city of Herat, a few miles across the border. Herat had at one point been regarded as part of Persia, but Afghani tribesmen had seized it in 1750. Eventually the English moved in, serving as protectors of the city because they believed it held strategic significance in the region and could serve as an overland gateway to India.

In response to Persia's attack on Herat, the English dispatched a fleet of warships from India to Kharg Island in the Persian Gulf, just off the western coast of Persia. From Kharg Island the English commander sent an ultimatum to Tehran, threatening to invade the kingdom unless the Qajar shah withdrew his army from Herat. The ultimatum read:

> If the Persian army does not [end] the siege of Herat, we shall occupy the whole coast of Fars, even the whole province. We shall change the friendship between Persia and England to enmity and do what will be appropriate and suitable.

Faced with the likelihood of military defeat, Mohammad Shah grudgingly complied. He never again tested the will of a foreign power.

The Bab

Qajar rulers would soon require the services of their army to keep peace at home. In 1844 a 25-year-old merchant named Mirza Ali Mohammad declared himself the mahdi, a messianic figure who some Muslims believe will create a world in accordance with the teachings of Allah. Mirza took the title Bab, which means "the gate." His followers offered ideas that alarmed the religious leaders of Persia, who were Shia Muslims. In a society in which females had to wear veils in public, the Bab preached equality for women and opposed the Islamic custom of taking multiple wives. In a society in which Sharia, which is the interpretation of Islamic law, required the hands of thieves to be cut off, the Bab preached moderation in punishment. He also called for better treatment of children and for begging to be outlawed. In Tehran, Islamic clerics advised Mohammad Shah that the Bab represented a danger to the country.

For three years Mohammad Shah tolerated the Bab because the self-proclaimed mahdi made few public pronouncements. In 1847, however, the Bab started calling for followers (Babis) to unite behind him. In 1848 the Bab preached before a large crowd in the city of Badasht, and one of his disciples, a woman named Qorrat al-'Ain, tore off her veil and urged people to reject the Qur'an, the holy scriptures of Islam. Qorrat al-'Ain promised that the Bab would write a new spiritual law. Mohammad Shah responded by having the Bab thrown into jail.

Before Mohammad Shah could act further, he died. When the Babis staged a series of small and ineffective yet troublesome uprisings, Mohammad Shah's successor, his son Nasser al-Din, hurried to Tehran where he hoped to restore order. Nasser al-Din decided that the best way to calm the Bab's angry followers was to eliminate their leader. In 1850 he ordered the execution of the Bab by a firing squad. But when the uprisings continued, Nasser al-Din sent troops to massacre the Bab's followers.

Strong Monarch

By eliminating the threat of Babism, Nasser al-Din managed to restore a sense of order to his kingdom. Still, wherever the young shah looked he found trouble. The regime of Mohammad Shah had left the national treasury bankrupt—corruption among the shah's advisors, a failure to collect taxes, and the ill-advised invasion of Herat in 1837 had depleted the state's coffers. Persia had also failed to keep up with modern developments. There were no modern roads or communication systems. The majority of Iranian people were unskilled and uneducated. The army was ill-equipped and poorly trained.

Nasser al-Din was 17 at the time of his coronation, but despite his young age he recognized that Persia needed to take advantage of the many advances in science, technology, and commerce that had appeared in the Western world. He began, with the help of prime ministers who advised him, to introduce reforms in both government and the larger Iranian society. The reforms were well intentioned, but they would fall short of modernizing Persia or improving the lives of most of its people.

Nasser al-Din's first prime minister, Amir Kabir, had been his tutor. It was at Amir Kabir's urging that Nasser al-Din had ordered the execution of the Bab and his followers. Amir Kabir believed that the show of force would establish the teenage shah as a strong monarch, thus discouraging acts of rebellion among other malcontents. Amir Kabir soon assumed control of the kingdom's treasury and its ineffective government bureaucracy.

Amir Kabir had hoped to institute major changes in Iran, such as the construction of new factories, roads, and communications systems. He also

English cavalry attacks Persian troops during the Anglo-Persian War of 1856–57. The conflict lasted just six months, and ended with a Persian agreement to withdraw from Herat.

wanted the government to build schools and introduce modern farming methods. Amir Kabir made little progress, though, because soon after taking office as prime minister he ran afoul of the shah's mother, Mahd Ulya. She convinced her son that Amir Kabir harbored unscrupulous intentions. In 1851 Nasser al-Din dismissed Amir Kabir, then had him arrested and exiled to a distant city. A few weeks later Amir Kabir was murdered by his guards.

Amir Kabir's place was taken by Mirza Agha Khan Nuri. He lasted seven years, until he was dismissed for advising Nasser al-Din to order another invasion of Herat. Persia succeeded in capturing Herat, but this in turn led to war with Great Britain, which wanted Afghanistan to remain independent as a way to check Russian expansion into Central Asia. Early in the Anglo-Persian War of 1856–57, the English occupied the port city of Bushehr on Iran's western coast. Two months later they defeated the Persian army at Kooshab. The 1857 treaty ending the war required the Iranians to renounce all claims to Herat or other land in Afghanistan. The shah agreed, and the English left Bushehr.

Opening Trade

After dismissing Nuri, Nasser al-Din elected to rule without the aid of a prime minister. He listened to many advisors, though, and one man soon emerged as an important voice for reform. He was Mirza Hosain Khan, a well-traveled diplomat whose greatest achievement, perhaps, was in convincing Nasser al-Din to travel beyond the borders of his kingdom. Eventually the shah would embark on three tours of European cities, where he could see for himself the benefits of education, industrialization, and modern communications. As a result of the shah's observations, in 1862 Persia's first telegraph line was constructed. Khan also took steps to stamp out the slave trade in Persia, which the British had demanded as part of the 1857 treaty. Also during this time Persia opened its first technical college, the Dar-ul-Fonun military academy, where students learned engineering, mathematics, and foreign languages. Wealthy Iranian families were encouraged to send their children to schools in Paris.

Under Khan the shah established ministries of justice and war, and he advanced improvements to the army. But Khan faced resistance to changes in the ministry of justice. In Iran, the courts operated under Sharia law, which means they were administered by clerics who often did not approve of the reforms suggested by the shah's bureaucrats.

Nasser al-Din considered Khan a close and trusted advisor, and in 1871 appointed him prime minister. This meant Khan could accelerate the pace of his reforms. He reorganized the government, ordering all ministers to meet weekly, and he established permanent offices for the ministries. Khan improved the training for the army by hiring a cadre of Austrian officers to drill the Persian troops. He also improved the postal service in Persia, again with help from Austrian advisors.

At Khan's urging, Nasser al-Din signed trade agreements with the Russians and English—pacts that helped thwart the Ottomans' western blockade. This

By signing trade agreements with Western countries, Nasser al-Din opened new markets for Persian goods such as this ornate carpet.

arrangement allowed Russian merchants to send goods into Persia south through the Caucasus Mountains, and the English to dock their ships at Persia's port cities or transport their goods overland through Afghanistan. Suddenly, British and Russian goods flooded Persia's markets. The Persians found themselves exporting goods as well. They found lucrative markets for their elegant handcrafted carpets throughout Europe. Persian merchants also shipped cotton, silk, tobacco, and opium to customers in Europe.

Although wealthy landowners prospered during this era, ordinary Persians continued to live marginal lives. In 1870 and 1871 an estimated 10 percent of the Persian population perished because of food shortages precipitated by a devastating drought. Persia had experienced droughts before, but this one was particularly deadly because much of the country's farmland had been replanted with cash crops headed for European markets.

The Reuter Concession

Both the Russians and the British welcomed better relations with Persia. England needed Persia to serve as a buffer between Russia and

Wealthy Persian landowners were outraged at the concessions granted to English businessman Paul Julius de Reuter, and pressured the shah to cancel the deal.

India, while Russia needed the Persians to guard their southern border along the Caucasus Mountains.

Khan trusted and favored the English. At his urging, in 1872 Nasser al-Din signed a deal with an English businessman, Paul Julius de Reuter—the founder of the Reuters news service—giving Reuter the rights to build a railroad through Persia. In exchange for building the railroad, the journalist would hold title to factories, canals, mines, farms, and other Persian resources. The value to Reuter was incalculable. Never before in history had a government turned over so much of its country's potential wealth to a private individual.

News of the so-called Reuter Concession spread throughout the ranks of Persia's wealthy landowners, who calculated that the deal would result in huge losses for them. The country's Islamic clergy also railed against the Reuter Concession, fuming that an outsider and non-Muslim would soon become the most influential man in Persia. In 1873 Nasser al-Din gave in to the pressure and canceled the deal with Reuter, who then ordered his workers to abandon the partially finished railroad.

Khan found himself singled out and maligned for the failed concession, and Nasser al-Din had no choice but to dismiss his close friend and advisor. Khan's dismissal as prime minister in 1873 meant the end to most Persian reforms. During the last two decades of Nasser al-Din's reign, the sultan preferred mostly to enjoy the luxuries of his rule. He lost touch with the Iranian people, whose problems mounted.

ودرت معارف اوزره مرتب علوم مکاتب رشدیه عسکریه شاهانه لرینك نواحی کشاورلری بیانیله معلوم بونمانه شاكردانه فرقدلری موجود و یمقدر جدول اولدر

محافظات	عدد	متنبهان اعضا	نواحی کشاورلری	محافظات	عدد	متنبهان اعضا	نواحی کشاورلری
نهایت	۱۸٤	شهر عسکریه	۱۲۹۸	یکی	٦٦٤	رشه یکسکریه	۱۴۰۰
,,	۱٤٤	,,	۱٤۰۷	نهایت	٦۷۰	,,	۱۲۹۷
,,	۵٥۱	,,	۱۲۹۷	,,	٦۹۹	,,	۱۲۹۷
یکی وضابط یکی	۰٦۹	,,	۱٤۰۵	,,	۰۹۰	,,	۱۲۹۷
,,	۱٤۸	,,	۱٤۰٤	,,	٤٤۵	,,	۱۲۹۷
نهایت	۰۵٤	,,	۱۲۹۷	,,	٤۸۸	,,	۱۲۹۷
,,	٦۰۷	,,	۱۲۹۷	,,	٤۷٤	,,	۱۲۹۷
,,	۱٦٤	,,	۱٤۰۱	,,	۰۰۰	,,	۱۲۹۷
,,	٦٤٦	,,	۱۲۹۷	,,	۰۸۹	,,	۱۲۹۸
,,	۱۸٦	,,	۱٤۰٦	,,	۱۷٦	,,	۱۴۰۰
,,	٤۷۵	,,	۱۲۹۸	,,	٦۹۷	,,	۱۲۹۸
,,	۱۷۹	,,	۱۲۹۸	,,	٤٤۱	,,	۱۲۹۸
,,	۱۱۹	,,	۱٤۰۹	,,	٤٤٤	,,	۱۲۹۹
		,,	۱٤۰۸	,,	٤۱٤	,,	۱۴۰۰
یکون	٤۱۸٤			یکون	۰۵٤۱۹		

During the Tanzimat reforms in the Ottoman Empire, many new hospitals, schools, and other public buildings were constructed. (Opposite) This Ottoman government record lists high-school attendance. (Right) The Hasköy Hospital for women, Istanbul.

4 *Reform in the Ottoman Empire*

y the late 1830s it was clear the Ottoman Empire was in decline. The imperial government was inefficient and corrupt. Unemployment was rising because of competition from cheap products imported from India and the Far East. The empire lacked decent roads and railways, modern methods of communication, and schools. And the destruction of the Ottoman navy at Navarino during the Greek War for Independence had shown that the Ottoman military, lacking proper training and modern weaponry, could no longer compete with the European powers.

Sultan Mahmud II recognized that the Ottoman Empire needed to change in order to compete with European powers. He provided the impetus for the Tanzimat reforms, although they were not implemented until after his death.

In 1830 Sultan Mahmud II took the unprecedented step of touring his realm. This was the first of five trips he would take over the next nine years to inspect industries, railways, forts, dockyards, and other institutions to survey what had gone wrong.

To bolster the empire, Mahmud envisioned the "reordering" of Ottoman society. He established a series of reforms that became known as the Tanzimat. Mahmud died in 1839, before the Tanzimat reforms could be instituted, but his son and successor, 16-year-old Abdulmecid I, continued his father's plans. Soon after his coronation, Abdulmecid appeared at a ceremony held in the Gülhane gardens of his palace, where he issued an edict making the Tanzimat part of Ottoman life.

Limited Reforms

The Tanzimat called for a system of fair taxation, outlawed bribery of public officials, standardized the country's penal code, and called for the empire's sizable population of non-Muslims to be granted the same rights as Muslims. But the reforms stopped short of instituting a new constitution or publicly elected parliament, which meant the sultan retained the right to exercise absolute power throughout the empire.

The one provision of the Tanzimat that most outraged Islamic clerics was the call for equal treatment of Muslims and non-Muslims. Under the Qur'an, Muslims—who are believers in Allah and the teachings of the Prophet Muhammad—are regarded as superior to non-Muslims. The rest of the Tanzimat was not easily enforced, either. Abdulmecid hoped to spread his reforms by publishing its terms in newspapers, but the majority of his subjects were illiterate. The empire was too vast and many people were too set in their ways to accept change easily. Government officials who were supposed to administer the reforms received no training. They were unsure how to apply the Tanzimat, so the implementation of the sultan's reforms varied from place to place.

Still Abdulmecid pressed on. At the urging of Great Britain the sultan closed down the country's slave markets, although slavery would persist well into the 20th century. The sultan also invited European artists and musicians to visit Constantinople; as a result, Italian music became popular among wealthy Turks. European architects added their touches to the Ottoman capital, and starting in 1851, Turkey sent exhibitors to world fairs in European cities, showing off Ottoman crafts, artwork, agricultural products, and textiles. In 1863, Constantinople hosted its first international exposition.

Sick Man of Europe

As Abdulmecid instituted his reforms, Russia continued to plot to acquire Ottoman lands. Tsar Nicholas I had taken power in the Russian Empire in 1825 after the death of his brother Alexander. During the 1850s Nicholas surveyed the state of the Ottoman regime and proclaimed it the "Sick Man of Europe"—a description the empire would bear until its final days.

Nicholas declared himself the protector of Christians living in the Ottoman Empire. In reality, he intended to seize Bulgaria and the Balkans states in eastern Europe, and he approved the invasion of Moldavia and Wallachia in 1853. The hostilities led to the Crimean War.

Thanks to the involvement of Britain and France, which joined the conflict on the Ottoman side, the Crimean War ended in defeat for Russia. The 1858 Treaty of Paris dictated the peace terms; the Ottomans emerged from the conflict with no further erosion of their empire, but the British insisted that internal reforms continue beyond the provisions of the Tanzimat. Among other things, British leaders insisted that conditions for non-Muslims be improved. High on the list of reforms was greater freedom for Christians to practice their religion within the empire. Abdulmecid agreed, and soon Islamic leaders were horrified to find Christian missionaries fanning out in Turkey and the Middle East seeking to convert Muslims.

Other changes were included in the so-called Reform Edict issued shortly after the Treaty of Paris. Abdulmecid reorganized the government, establishing new ministries to manage public works, justice, education, finance,

British and Russian troops clash during the Battle of Balaklava, 1855. France and Great Britain supported the Ottoman Empire during the Crimean War; in exchange the sultan agreed to additional reforms within the empire.

agriculture, trade, and the military. Jobs in those ministries were made available to non-Muslims. Islamic leaders found this move repugnant as well, particularly when it came to placing non-Muslims in influential positions in the justice and education ministries. Under Islamic law, education and the courts had always been the responsibilities of the clerics.

There was one final outcome of the Crimean War that would haunt the Ottoman rulers for years to come. To finance the war, Abdulmecid had borrowed money from European banks. At the end of the hostilities, Abdulmecid managed to keep his empire intact, but the cost was an enormous debt. In later years other sultans would also be forced to appeal to foreign interests for financial aid. Eventually, the huge loans crippled the Ottomans. By the 1870s about 80 percent of the taxes collected by the Ottoman rulers were handed over to the empire's creditors.

The Spread of Nationalism

Ottoman leaders believed that reforms granting more rights to Christians, Jews, and others would seal their loyalty to the Ottoman Empire. That did not happen, however. Despite the reforms of the Tanzimat period, Bulgarians, Serbians, Macedonians, and others under Ottoman rule in eastern Europe wanted to govern themselves. The spirit of nationalism was further ignited by a drought and famine that struck the empire in 1873. The catastrophe left thousands dead and homeless, and the loss cost the Ottoman government significant tax revenue. To make up for shortfall, the sultan ordered new taxes levied on his Slavic subjects in eastern Europe, which deepened resentments against him.

Meanwhile, a spirit of nationalism had started to take hold not only in eastern European lands under Ottoman control but elsewhere as well. In 1860 civil war broke out in the Ottoman-held territory of Lebanon in the Middle East. Thousands died in the fighting. The Ottomans dispatched soldiers to maintain peace, which they accomplished using brute force. Then in 1884, a nationalist uprising in Sudan defeated the occupying Ottoman Egyptian and British armies.

Abdulmecid did not live to see the further disintegration of his empire. He died of tuberculosis in 1861 and was succeeded by a younger brother, Abdulaziz. Like his father and brother, Abdulaziz was determined to carry out the Tanzimat reforms. He authorized construction of new railroads and roads, and extended telegraph lines throughout the empire. During the reign of his predecessor Abdulmecid, a few new schools had been opened—mostly technical academies designed to train future military officers. But Abdulaziz took matters a step further, building primary and secondary schools aimed at educating the children of ordinary citizens. The building program was expensive—to finance the schools, Abdulaziz and his successors borrowed heavily from foreign powers, digging the empire deeper into debt. In addition, other than clerics there were few trained teachers available to work in the schools.

Abdulaziz also spent heavily on the Ottoman fleet. He authorized construction of nearly 80 navy vessels, including 20 battleships. To finance the new fleet, he borrowed money yet again.

By 1871 the cost of the Tanzimat as well as the modernization of the railroads, telegraph system, roads, and navy had taken its toll on the national treasury. Still saddled with its debt from the Crimean War, the government had run out of money. It could no longer pay off its foreign debt. And the little investment that foreign banks and businesses had made suddenly dried up.

The Young Ottomans

In the 1860s a movement emerged among poets, writers, and other intellectuals who believed that the empire could adopt the democratic reforms found in England, France, and elsewhere in Europe. The activists, who came to be known as the Young Ottomans, believed that establishment of a constitution and a democratically elected parliament could also help defuse tensions between the empire's Muslims and non-Muslims. They believed strongly that Islam could be incorporated into the new government. They also believed that a parliament could do a better job of managing the empire than the sultan.

Over the years the Young Ottomans published their ideas in newspapers, which were tolerated under the Tanzimat reforms. They soon generated a following, which included high-ranking officials in the sultan's government. By 1876 a group of conspirators made plans to topple Abdulaziz and install his son Murad, as sultan. Murad supported the plot and had agreed to the establishment of a constitutional monarchy with many of the sultan's powers assumed by a parliament. The conspirators made their move on May 30. The coup d'etat was bloodless; Abdulaziz was placed under house arrest, while his 26-year-old son took control of the government.

Abdulaziz died a few days later. However, Murad would reign as sultan for just two months, because he proved to be mentally ill. On August 31, 1876, leaders of the Young Turks engineered Murad's ouster. The sultan's brother, Abdulhamid II, was next to take the throne.

Like Murad, Abdulhamid agreed to the establishment of a constitution and parliament. A constitution was written in the final few months of 1876, and the Ottoman empire's first democratic government became effective on March 19, 1877. But it would not last long. A month later, Russia made another move against the empire, invading Bulgaria. The Russo-Turkish War was brief, lasting less than a year. Wherever the armies clashed, the Russians

Sultan Abdulhamid II (1842–1918) initially agreed to allow a constitution to be written and a parliament to be formed. However, he soon suspended the constitution and ended the reform period, ruling with a heavy hand in order to keep the many elements of Ottoman society in line.

crushed the Ottoman defenders. In 1878 the Ottomans were forced to accept devastating peace terms under the Treaty of Berlin. Under the treaty, the Ottomans lost two-thirds of Bulgaria to the Russians and to an autonomous Bulgarian government. In the Balkans, the Ottomans lost Bosnia and Herzegovina to Austria-Hungary. Serbia and Montenegro also won their independence, although they would soon fall under domination by Austria-Hungary. Romania was next in line to win its independence. Great Britain took control of Cyprus, a strategically important island in the eastern Mediterranean Sea. The war with Russia cost the Ottomans 8 percent of their territory and some 4.5 million people, representing 20 percent of the empire's prewar population.

On February 14, 1878, not quite 11 months after the birth of Ottoman democracy, a bitter Abdulhamid suspended the constitution and closed down the parliament. He blamed the Tanzimat reforms for his nation's troubles and felt strongly that he could salvage what was left of his empire by reinstituting an authoritarian rule.

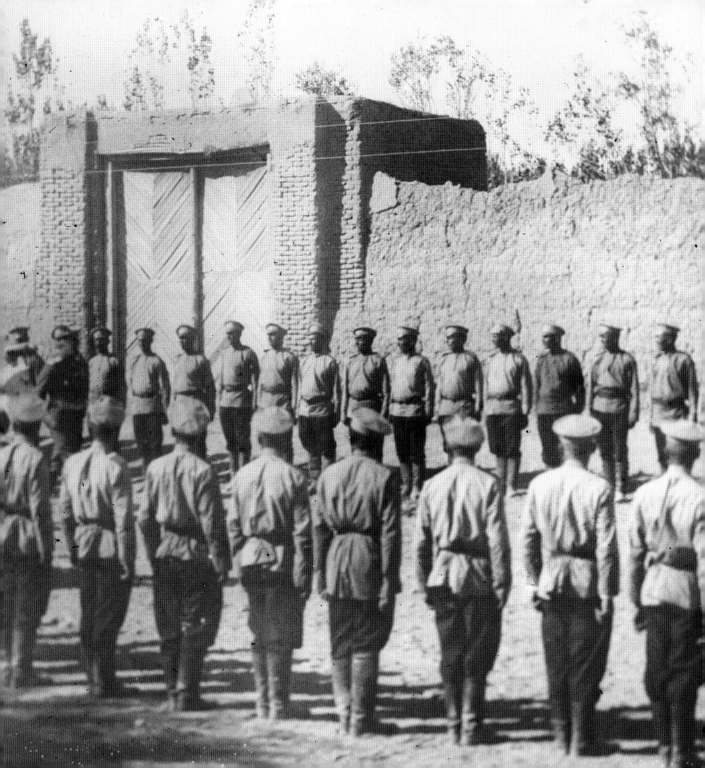

In the early years of the 20th century Persia was torn by internal political strife and foreign occupation. (Opposite) Russian soldiers stand at attention in Tehran, circa 1908. (Right) Religious leaders like these clerics pressed for Islam to have a greater role in the Persian government.

5 *Decline of the Qajar Empire*

espite the failure of the Reuter Concession, in the final years of his reign over Persia Nasser al-Din signed a number of deals with Russian and English businessmen, trading his country's resources for huge amounts of cash. Although money poured into the country from these deals, none filtered down to ordinary Persians. Nasser al-Din's people lived in poverty while he enjoyed a life of extreme luxury in an ornate palace, and he presided over his empire seated atop what became known as the Peacock Throne, a jewel-encrusted symbol of Qajar wealth.

Nasser al-Din traveled frequently to Europe, accompanied by an entourage of diplomats, guards, and wives. There, he spent lavishly on art, clothes, and furnishings. By the 1880s the shah no longer dressed in traditional Iranian robes and tunics. Instead, he wore finely tailored European suits.

To finance his extravagant lifestyle during the final few years of his reign, Nasser al-Din sold Persia's mining rights, permitted Russian and English banks to open in Tehran and elsewhere in the country, and found other businessmen willing to finance construction of a railroad. As Persians watched the wealth of their country pour into the pockets of foreigners, the more vocal among them started meeting in secret, where they voiced their complaints about the shah and his free-spending ways. Persia had always been a country of diverse peoples, but now members of different tribes, often at odds with one another, found themselves united against the shah and the dismal economic circumstances in which they lived.

The final straw for Persian dissidents was the shah's decision in 1890 to sell all rights to their country's tobacco to the British Imperial Tobacco Company. Tobacco was the one crop that touched the lives of nearly all Persians. Most men smoked tobacco, tens of thousands of peasants labored to grow the crop, and thousands of merchants made their livings by selling tobacco. The shah's decision to wrest control of the national crop out of the hands of the people led to protests throughout the country. Clerics preaching in their mosques denounced the deal. By the end of 1891, the peasants refused to work in the tobacco fields, merchants refused to sell tobacco products, and nearly everyone stopped smoking. In January 1892, Nasser al-Din grudgingly canceled the tobacco concession.

The Constitutional Revolution

Widespread protests continued unabated, culminating in the shah's murder on May 1, 1896. The assassin, Mirza Reza, was a disciple of Jamal ed-Din Afghani, a cleric who had been among the earliest and most vocal opponents of Western influence in Persia. Nasser al-Din had expelled Afghani from the country in 1891. Mirza Reza, who had spent time in Persian prisons, shot Nasser al-Din at a Tehran mosque; Afghani had urged him to carry out the crime, for which Mirza Reza was later hanged.

The new shah, Nasser al-Din's 43-year-old son Muzaffar al-Din, soon proved to be incompetent, corrupt, and as extravagant with his spending as his father. By 1905, with Persia even deeper in debt, protests again started erupting throughout the country, sparked by bread shortages and crop failures.

A French magazine pictures Muzaffar al-Din (1853–1907) shortly after he succeeded his father as shah in 1896. Under both domestic and foreign pressure, he permitted a constitution to be drafted and authorized the creation of a parliament called the majlis.

During this period of protest, three leaders emerged: Muhammad Tabatabai, Abdullah Behbahani, and Sheikh Fazollah Nuri. Each preached against Western influences in Persia, and advocated a new direction. They called for a constitution and for the shah to share power with a parliament, or majlis. They sparked a movement that became known as the Constitutional Revolution. Writers and other Persian intellectuals hoped to model the constitution on the democratic ideals espoused in western European nations, while the clerics wanted it to be based on Islamic law. The clerics had an advantage because they spoke directly to large numbers of people in their mosques. Although the writers argued for their ideas in literary journals, most Persians could not read these publications.

Embassy Standoff

Less than 10 years after he had ascended to the Persian throne, Muzaffar al-Din was driven from power. His departure was precipitated by his prime minister, Ain al-Dawla. When Ain al-Dawla raised the price of sugar in the country, protests broke out immediately. Merchants closed the bazaars, and as word spread through Tehran, thousands of people took to the streets and gathered around one of Tehran's largest mosques. Muzaffar dispatched troops to quell the disturbance, but his men soon found themselves outnumbered. The protest ended peacefully when Muzaffar reluctantly promised to fire his prime minister and establish a majlis.

Months passed with the shah taking no action. Muzaffar had fallen ill and was close to death. Tabatabai, Behbahani, and Nuri stirred up passions by calling for revolution. From his mosque, Tabatabai thundered, "We want justice, we want a majlis in which the shah and the beggar are equal before the law!"

In response Ain al-Dawla imposed a curfew on Tehran. When protesters broke the curfew and filled city streets, the prime minister dispatched troops to disperse the crowds. On the night of June 17, 1906, the shah's troops fired into the crowd, killing a man. The martyr's funeral was attended by thousands; Behbahani led the prayers.

Tehran merchants closed the city's bazaars as an act of continued protest, in defiance of an order by Ain al-Dawla to keep the stores open. Seeking protection, hundreds of merchants appealed for sanctuary within the walls of the British embassy in Tehran. They were followed by others, and soon 20,000 Iranians were camped in tents on the grounds of the embassy. Others found sanctuary within the walls of the Russian embassy. By now, both the British and Russian governments had concluded that the Qajar regime was in crisis.

The standoff lasted a month. The ailing Muzaffar found himself pressured not only by his own subjects but by the British and Russians to concede to the protesters' demands. Finally, he agreed to their terms: establishment of a majlis and the drafting of a constitution. On October 7, 1906, a new era of Iranian democracy commenced when the majlis convened its first session. Muzaffar died three months later, just after signing the constitution.

Internal Dissent

The majlis was dominated by liberal intellectuals. The constitution they produced reduced the role of Islam in the lives of Persians. For example, the constitution recognized equal treatment under the law for non-Muslims, and it stipulated the administration of fair justice, which was contrary to the Sharia, which held that a cleric could administer justice based on his interpretation of the Qur'an. The new constitution also called for the establishment of public schools; previously, education had always been under the authority of the Islamic clergy.

Clerics in the majlis reacted to these liberal reforms by demanding more of a voice. They hoped was that a committee of religious scholars could hold veto power over legislation that was judged to be against Islamic teachings. The liberals in the majlis agreed, but then refused to appoint the committee. Sensing an opportunity in this division, the new shah, Muzaffar's 34-year-old son Mohammad Ali Mirzi, threatened to close down the majlis.

Observing all this rather closely were the Russians and British, who concluded that Iran seemed incapable of maintaining a democracy. Meeting secretly in 1907, Russian and British officials planned to carve up the country when the inevitable civil war finally broke out. The Anglo-Russian Pact of 1907 essentially split the country into two halves, with the Russians overseeing the northern half and the British maintaining a presence in the southern half. With the details worked out, the two powers waited for the appropriate moment to carry out their plan.

Failure of Democracy

That moment arrived on June 23, 1908. With the majlis frozen by dissent and with civil order close to breaking down, the shah appealed to the Russian military to take charge. Russian soldiers entered Tehran and surrounded the legislative building as well as a neighboring mosque. For six hours, the Russians fired their guns into the building, until finally, all legislators inside had surrendered. The survivors were arrested and some were executed on the shah's orders.

Shah Mohammad Ali Mirzi (1872–1925) opposed the majlis, and with the help of Russian troops he eliminated the parliament in 1908. This did not end the Constitutional Revolution, however, and the shah was forced to abdicate the next year.

The Constitutional Revolution was not yet over, however. Persian rebels held out across the country. Many, near starvation, fought hard against the Russian troops. By July 1909 the rebels regrouped and launched an assault on Tehran. By now, the British and Russians had lost confidence in Mohammad Ali and decided to let the rebels take the city. The shah sought refuge in the Russian embassy and abdicated.

It had never been the intention of the rebels to end the Qajar regime. With Mohammad Ali Mirzi giving up the throne the rebels accepted his 12-

Ahmad Shah Qajar (1898–1930) was just 12 years old when he replaced his father as ruler of Persia in 1909. He proved to be an ineffective ruler, and was the last Qajar shah of Persia.

year-old son, Ahmad, as shah. The majlis reconvened, but the parliament was plagued by dissent and an inability to solve disputes. Few reforms were enacted, and virtually nothing the legislators enacted improved the lives of ordinary Iranians. In her book *The Iranians: Persia, Islam and the Soul of a Nation*, historian Sandra Mackey observed:

> The Constitutionalists lost the revolution because the traditionalists of the [clergy] refused to allow the Iranians to adopt ideas and methods that could help address the monumental problems that stood between Iran and the 20th century. At the other extreme, the modernizers who so enthusiastically embraced Western ideas failed to recognize that modernization in an exclusively Western mode demanded the same values and attitudes that underlay Western culture and advancement. In the Iran of Persia and Islam these did not exist.

Constitutional government in Iran drew its final breath on December 24, 1911, when Russian troops, at the request of the young shah's advisors, closed down the majlis.

The pace of reform quickened in the Ottoman Empire during the first decades of the 20th century. (Opposite) King Nicholas of Montenegro reviews troops during the Balkan War, October 1912. (Right) Members of the Committee of Union and Progress, a political party that dominated parliament between 1908 and 1918.

6 The Young Turks Gain Power

In the decade after Sultan Abdulhamid II closed down the Ottoman parliament and reasserted his authority, a widespread movement to return democracy to the empire found support among intellectuals, clerics, government officials, and others. Revolutionaries started meeting in secret, but as soon as Abdulhamid learned of their activities, he clamped down on dissent. Many of the movement's leaders fled to Paris, where they could continue their organizational activities in public. In 1894 elements of the opposition came together under a single umbrella organization known as the

Committee of Union and Progress, or CUP. Leaders of CUP became more widely known as the "Young Turks."

There were many elements of Ottoman society that opposed Abdulhamid's rule. Armenians, Macedonians, Arabs, Kurds, and other nationalities craved independence. Throughout the empire, occasional revolts against taxation and mandatory military conscription erupted.

By the early 1900s CUP leaders were publicly calling for the reestablishment of the constitution of 1876. They also approached influential officers in the Ottoman army who could further their revolutionary plans. One young officer, Major Ismail Enver, would soon emerge as one of the military's most influential CUP leaders.

Support for the ideals of the Committee of Union and Progress spread quickly through Macedonia, where each city and tiny village seemed to have its own cell of revolutionaries. By 1903 settlement of the "Macedonian Question"—the liberation of the Balkan state—was the most pressing crisis in Abdulhamid's reign. His ministers calmed revolutionary fervor in Macedonia by asking Russia and Austria-Hungary to be responsible for preserving peace and security in the region. However, this move also encouraged opponents of the imperial government because it limited Ottoman authority in the Balkans.

By 1908 the CUP operated openly throughout the empire despite the sultan's continuing campaign to jail its leaders. In Macedonia, outright rebellion broke out with armed civilians calling for a return to constitutional government. An Ottoman army led by Major Enver backed the rebels, and on July 23 took control of the Macedonian government. The new government in Macedonia announced it had reinstituted the constitution and threatened an attack on Constantinople unless the sultan agreed to share his rule with a parliament. A day later, realizing that he

Ismail Enver (1881–1922) was one of the most powerful leaders of the Committee of Union and Progress. He acted as de facto ruler of the Ottoman Empire for six turbulent years, from 1913 to 1918.

faced armed rebellion in the streets of Istanbul, Abdulhamid agreed to the CUP's demands.

As the Young Turks prepared to take power in Constantinople, the empire disintegrated further, hastened in no small part by foreign powers anxious to profit from the instability of the Ottoman government. In October the remaining Ottoman territory in Bulgaria joined the independent Bulgarian state. The island of Crete in the Mediterranean Sea broke away as well, announcing its unification with Greece. Austria-Hungary, which had been awarded Bosnia and Herzegovina under the Treaty of Berlin, announced its formal annexation of the two Balkans states.

The March 31 Incident

Finally, after hastily arranged elections, the Ottoman parliament reconvened on December 17, 1908, with CUP candidates winning most of the seats. But the elections failed to secure peace and stability. Soon an estimated 250,000 factory workers went on strike. For centuries, workers had enjoyed virtually no rights in the Ottoman Empire. Now, with a democratic government in power, the workers started demanding rights. Liberal intellectuals welcomed the strikes, proclaiming that the workers were finally free of the sultan's authoritarian rule; nevertheless, for the first few months of 1909, the already fragile Ottoman economy suffered further as factory production ground to a standstill.

Problems plagued the parliament as well. Islamic clerics did not control enough seats in parliament to sway legislation and complained that the CUP leaders were as authoritarian as the sultan. For example, the CUP-controlled parliament passed a law permitting women to attend Ottoman universities—an insult to conservative followers of Islam. Soon, the clerics formed an organization they called the Muslim Union and started agitating for revolt against the CUP. They found allies among devout Muslims in the army. They also found an ally in Abdulhamid, who promised that with the Young Turks out of power he would rule in accordance with Islamic law.

The conspirators moved on March 31, 1909. During the so-called Incident of March 31, CUP-allied army officers were taken prisoners by their men, who then surrounded the parliament building. The rebels forced the CUP leaders in parliament to resign.

Rule under the countercoup was brief. The CUP still had many allies in the army, one of whom was a high-ranking officer, Mahmud Sevket Pasha. Mahmud Sevket rushed his troops to Constantinople, where they took control of the sultan's palace. They were joined by a delegation of CUP leaders, who demanded Abdulhamid's abdication. On April 27, 1909, Abdulhamid was escorted out of the palace and replaced as sultan by his brother, Mehmed V. Mahmud Sevket's troops also ousted the Muslim Union from parliament—some 80 Muslim Union leaders, including 50 army officers, were arrested and hanged.

The CUP emerged from the March 31 Incident back in power and determined to assert its authority. CUP leaders decided the constitution of 1876 was outdated and needed to be rewritten. They delivered a new constitution that stripped away many of the sultan's powers. Soon, the Young Turks resorted to violent means to take control of the empire. Said historian S.L.A. Marshall in his book, *The American Heritage History of World War I,*

> It was supposed to have been a cleansing democratic reform. The ideal has seldom anywhere been more hideously mocked and degraded. In office, these men behaved like the worst of the Chicago mobs in Prohibition days, using murder, torture, and terror to consolidate their gains. Massacres of minority groups and wholesale deportations were common. Opponents, that is, all who dared protest, were garroted or hanged. It was a government with character—all bad.

The CUP leaders faced many challenges, both inside and outside the empire. Following the countercoup, parliament appointed Mahmud Sevket as head of the Ottoman military, and he soon rose to a position of power in Ottoman government.

Turmoil continued to plague the empire in the first decades of the 20th century. In 1911 the Italian army seized the Ottoman-held territory in North Africa known as Tripoli. (Today it is part of Libya.) Nationalism was again on the rise in the Balkans where agitators—spurred on by Russia—called for independence from the Ottomans. Inside the empire the CUP won parliamentary elections in early 1912, but many of the seats were alleged to have been captured through electoral fraud. Under pressure from the army, Mehmed called on parliament to stage new elections. Before the elections could be staged, however, hostilities in the Balkans reached a fever pitch. That October, the First Balkan War was underway.

The Balkan Wars

Although the Ottomans had been steadily losing territory in the Balkans since the 1830s, by the eve of the First Balkan War the empire still controlled Albania, Macedonia, and the region known as Thrace. With near-chaos reigning in Constantinople, two other Balkan states, Serbia and Montenegro, along with neighboring Greece and Bulgaria—all with the encouragement of Russia—saw their opportunity to finally rid the Balkan peninsula of Ottoman authority. The first blow in the war was struck on October 8 by Montenegro, which attacked an Ottoman fort in the Albanian city of Shkodër. Bulgaria, Greece, and Serbia quickly joined the fight, amassing a combined army of some 750,000 men. By December, the armies of the Balkan states succeeded in driving back the Ottoman army. With the Balkan armies just 30 miles from Constantinople, the Ottomans called for a ceasefire and sent diplomats to London to listen to the demands of the Balkan leaders.

Back in Constantinople the capital was characterized by chaos. On January 23, 1913, Ismail Enver, leading a contingent of troops, assassinated the minister of war and forced the prime minister to resign at gunpoint. Next, Enver forced Mehmed to appoint Mahmud Sevket the new prime minister.

In London the Ottomans conceded control over all their remaining territories in eastern Europe. Mahmud Sevket at first rejected the demands and ordered an attack on the Bulgarian army in the city of Edirne in Thrace. When the Bulgarians easily beat back the attack, Sevket reluctantly agreed to the terms. The peace treaty was signed on May 30, 1913. Twelve days later, Mahmud Sevket was assassinated.

Mehmed Talat Pasha (1874–1921) was among the most important leaders of the Young Turk movement in the early 20th century.

In Constantinople the CUP leaders in parliament labored to stabilize the government. An ally of Enver, Mehmed Talat Pasha, a former postal employee who had been among the earliest CUP organizers, was appointed prime minister.

Within months, hostilities flared in the Balkans again as the one-time allies fought among themselves over how to split up the territory lost by the

Ottomans. Taking advantage of the situation, Enver led an Ottoman army back into Edirne, retaking it from the Bulgarians.

The Second Balkan War lasted until August 1913. Eventually, borders within the Balkan states shifted as the much stronger powers of Austria-Hungary and Germany exerted their dominance over Serbia, Bulgaria, and the other nations in the region. Over the next 12 months, the unsettled situation in the Balkans would lead to a much wider war that would draw in virtually every other country in Europe as well as the Middle East and eventually the United States. World War I was on the horizon, and it would prove to have disastrous consequences for the Ottoman Empire.

LEST THEY PERISH

World War I was the death knell for both the Ottoman and Qajar dynasties. (Opposite) Detail from a poster promoting aid to Armenians, who were persecuted by the Ottoman government during the war. (Right) Ottoman troops camped in the hills of Gallipoli. In 1915 the Turks successfully fought off a British assault on the peninsula.

7 The First World War and its Aftermath

In August 1914 war broke out in Europe. Great Britain, France, and Russia (the Allies) found themselves pitted against the Central Powers, primarily Germany, Austria-Hungary, and the Ottoman Empire. Persia declared its neutrality at the start of the war but was later drawn into the world conflict, as was the United States and many other nations. World War I, as this conflict came to be known, marked the first time in world history that so many countries took up arms at the same time.

Turkish Triumphs and Defeats

As the war commenced, Germany desperately needed the Ottoman Empire on their side because the empire controlled the Dardanelles, the strategically important straits that link the Aegean Sea off the coast of Greece with the Mamara Sea. If the Allies gained control of the Dardanelles, they could land troops and supplies to help Russia wage war against Germany and Austria-Hungary. The Ottoman rulers negotiated a favorable agreement with Germany in exchange for joining the Central Powers in October 1914.

Beginning in April 1915 the British attempted to capture the Dardanelles by attacking Ottoman positions on the Gallipoli peninsula. The Ottoman troops were bombarded by the Royal Navy while thousands of Allied troops, mostly Australians and New Zealanders, attempted to seize the beaches. The Gallipoli campaign proved to be a failure, resulting in more than 140,000 Allied soldiers killed or wounded. By January 1916 the Allies were forced to withdraw.

The Ottomans also scored a decisive victory in the Middle East, defeating a British army at Baghdad in 1916. The 10,000 British troops held out for nearly five months but finally found themselves overcome by malaria, dehydration, and an enemy of superior size.

After the defeat at Baghdad, the British changed their strategy. British intelligence officers prompted the leaders of the nomadic Arab tribes of the Middle East to stage what became known as the Great Arab Revolt. Ensured by the British that they would rule autonomous nations following the war—a promise that was ultimately broken—Arab chieftains

Bedouin soldiers gather in a small village in the Jordan Valley. In exchange for revolting against Ottoman rule in the Middle East, the Arabs were promised independence once the war ended.

conducted an effective guerilla war against the Ottoman Turks. British officer T.E. Lawrence helped organize the Arabs and lead them on their campaign to blow up Ottoman railroads and supply lines. The Arabs were not strong enough to oust the Ottoman Turks on their own, but they helped distract the Ottoman army, enabling the British to mount more effective offensives in the Middle East.

Perhaps the darkest page in the history of World War I occurred in Armenia, just west of Turkey. Concerned that the Christian Armenians living near the border with Russia would help Russian troops invade the empire, in 1915 the Ottomans began moving Armenians away from their homes. This deportation turned into a horrific genocide, in which Armenians were murdered by Turkish troops. Some estimates indicate that the Armenian death toll may have been as high as 1.2 million.

Persia During the War

The last Qajar shah, Ahmad, was just 16 years old when World War I began in August 1914. He spent most of the war years enriching his own pockets while concerned mostly with his own safety. In December 1914 the Persian political parties reconvened the majlis and immediately declared Persia's neutrality. But attempts to keep Persia out of the war were futile, especially after the Ottomans invaded Persian territory.

The Russians responded to the Ottoman invasion by crossing the Caucasus Mountains, entering Persia from the north. Over the course of the war, the two armies clashed several times in western Persia. Finally, in 1917 Russian troops were withdrawn by the new Bolshevik government, which had deposed the tsar and gained control of Russia.

In the south the British organized the South Persia Rifles, composed mostly of their own troops as well as fighters from India and members of the Persian cavalry. The British were primarily concerned with cutting off an Ottoman advance east toward Afghanistan and India, but they also valued the oil reserves that had been discovered in Iran. In 1912, the British fleet had begun using oil as fuel, rather than coal, because it offered many advantages. It was easier to load and store on ships, and was a more efficient fuel that would allow warships to travel faster and farther than coal-fueled ships could. However, a disadvantage was that Britain possessed large coal fields but no oil of its own, so the British desperately needed access to Persia's oil.

During the First World War British troops protected the oil fields of Persia, which held great strategic importance to the British war effort. Persia's oil was the lifeblood of the British Navy, which was needed to protect India and other colonies of the far-flung British Empire.

Persia suffered major losses during the war, even though the country contributed virtually nothing to the military campaign. Hundreds of thousands of Persian civilians died in the crossfire, and survivors found themselves living on the streets or in crude, squalid tent villages. Persia's cities lacked food, clean water, and medicine, and modern communications systems and transportation were virtually nonexistent. Supplies were ferried from city to city on the backs of camels. And, perhaps worst of all, at the end of the war, Persia found itself occupied by the British army. Said historian Nikki R. Kedde, author of the book, *Qajar Iran and the Rise of Reza Khan*,

> Iran came out ruined and in virtual anarchy from a war that it had officially refused to enter. Agricultural production fell, foreign troops used and disrupted supplies, and speculators worsened shortages. In 1917–18, it underwent a famine so grave that some ate tree roots and cannibalism was reported. The influenza epidemic, which ravaged Europe, brought tens of thousands of further deaths. Typhus was everywhere, and the total number of deaths from disease and famine was huge. Trade was disorganized and the price of wheat kept rising in Tehran while grain spoiled in silos elsewhere. Roads were ruined, bridges destroyed, and brigandage spread.

Birth of a New Dynasty

From this chaos emerged Reza Khan, a military officer from humble origins who had distinguished himself as a strong leader. Despite sizeable loans made by the British government, by 1921 conditions in Persia had not improved. At that point, Reza Khan decided to take control of the government. On February 21 he led 3,000 cavalry troops into Tehran, where he arrested the shah's cabinet and forced Ahmad to appoint him head of the military. He soon had himself appointed prime minister as well. The British chose not to intervene. In Reza Khan, they saw the one man who could stabilize the troubled country. Also, Reza Khan harbored a deep hatred for Russia's Bolshevik government—in 1921 he personally led a defense of the country against an ill-planned Bolshevik invasion—so the British were confident that

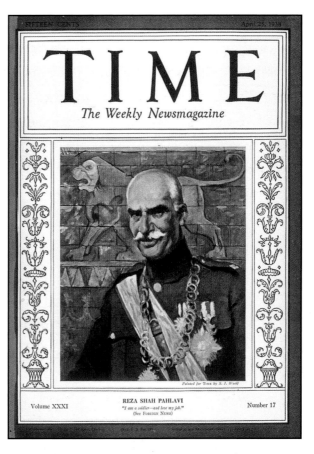

Reza Khan (1878–1944) assumed power in a military coup that deposed the last Qajar shah. Although he attempted to reform Persian society, his efforts left many people worse off then they had been in the Qajar period.

under Reza Khan, Persia would remain friendly to British interests.

The new leader of the country had no more use for a Qajar shah. Reza Khan planned to establish a republic, modeled after the democracies of western Europe. He faced opposition from Islamic clerics, however, as they once again raised their old fears about losing a voice in a secular government. And so Reza Khan struck a deal with the Islamic leaders of Persia: he would reign as shah, basing his government on the principles of Sharia law.

On October 31, 1925, the majlis—now no more than an instrument under the control of Reza Khan—deposed Ahmad from the Peacock Throne. The family that had unified Persia in the closing years of the 18th century was now out of power. Exiled to Paris, Ahmad Shah died five years later on February 21, 1930.

The Last Sultan

The Ottomans suffered huge losses in the war as well. By the end of the fighting, it was estimated that more than a million Turks had lost their lives. Under the Treaty of Versailles, the Ottoman empire was stripped of all territory beyond part of the Anatolian peninsula. Allied troops occupied Istanbul, where they rounded up the leaders of the Committee of Union and Progress (CUP) and tried them for wartime atrocities, particularly the genocide in Armenia. The two leaders of the wartime empire, Ismail Enver and Mehmed Talat, escaped before the end of the war. Both were tried in absentia and sentenced to death. Enver was killed by Bolshevik troops in Turkistan while trying to start a revolution against Russian rule, while Talat was assassinated while living in a small German village, possibly by an Armenian seeking revenge.

Although the Ottoman Empire was no more, Turkish nationalists fought to establish their independence from Allied control. During a three-year-long military campaign, a World War I hero named Mustafa Kemal managed to establish the borders of a new state, Turkey, which was larger than the Allies had originally planned. Kemal and his followers abolished the position of sultan on November 1, 1922, and the Republic of Turkey was

Mustafa Kemal Ataturk (1881–1938) is considered the father of modern Turkey. His policies established Turkey as a modern, secular state with a government based on Western democratic principles.

officially proclaimed on October 29, 1923. The 35th and last Ottoman sultan, Mehmed VI, was exiled from Turkey in 1924, ending more than 600 years of Ottoman rule. Kemal, who later took the surname Atatürk ("father of the Turks"), became Turkey's first president.

Atatürk and the new National Assembly drafted a constitution establishing a secular government. The Islamic clerics opposed the new laws, and so did others, particularly the Kurds, who felt their rights had been neglected in the new constitution. A minor rebellion flared up in 1924, but with the help of the British, Atatürk's government soon stamped out the crisis.

Different Paths

In the years following the fall of the Qajar and Ottoman regimes, Persia and Turkey followed different paths. In Persia the government chose a path of authoritarianism, providing Reza Khan with overwhelming powers over the lives of ordinary Iranians. In 1935 Reza Khan formally changed the country's name to Iran. In 1941 British and Russian fears that the shah would align Iran with Nazi Germany led to his removal from power, and his son Mohammad Reza Pahlavi became the new shah.

In 1979 radical Islamic clerics organized a revolution to depose Reza Pahlavi, prompted by the shah's despotic attitude toward his people. Since unseating Reza Pahlavi, Iran has followed a controversial and dangerous path, often challenging Western powers like the United States. The U.S. has accused Iran of secretly supporting terrorism in the Middle East as well as undertaking a program to develop nuclear weapons. Today, Iran is governed by a fundamentalist Islamic set of laws that has changed little since the days of the Qajar shahs—women still wear veils, non-Muslims are persecuted, and the regime is dedicated to spreading its radical ideas outside Iran.

In contrast Turkey has emerged as a stable democracy and an ally of the United States, although it is not without its problems. These include the sometimes-violent efforts of Kurds to break away and form their own state. However, for the most part Turkey has adapted to the challenges of maintaining order in the most volatile corner of the planet, the Middle East.

1299: Osman I unites Anatolia under his rule, giving birth to the Ottoman empire. At its height the Ottomans rule an empire of some 35 million people that includes territory in Eastern Europe, North Africa and the Middle East.

1796: Agha Muhammad Khan, the first Qajar shah, unites Iran after a 15-year civil war.

1798: On July 1 French troops seize Egypt from Ottomans; the French withdraw after three years following several military setbacks.

1804: A Persian army invades Georgia to seize the territory from Russia; after nine years of fighting, the Persians withdraw.

1805: Ottoman governor Muhammad Ali begins his 44-year reign over Egypt.

1826: Persia invades Georgia, but is again repelled by Russian troops.

1827: On October 20 the Ottoman navy is destroyed at the Battle of Navarino, the decisive event of the Greek war of independence.

1830: France annexes the Ottoman territory of Algeria.

1837: Mohammad Shah Qajar orders an attack on British-held Herat in Afghanistan; the army withdraws after England threatens to invade Persia.

1839: On November 3 Sultan Abdulmecid issues the Gülhane Edict, launching the Tanzimat reforms in the Ottoman empire.

1848: Nasser al-Din begins 48-year reign as shah of Iran.

1850: Nasser al-Din orders execution of a religious leader known as the Bab; thousands of the Bab's followers are also massacred.

1856: The Anglo-Persian War begins after Persia invades Herat a second time; the war ends a year later with a Persian defeat.

1865: The Young Ottoman movement, seeking a constitutional government in Turkey, is born.

1870: An estimated 10 percent of the population of Persia dies as a result of food shortages caused by a severe drought.

1872: Nasser al-Din signs the Reuter Concession, turning over vast resources in Persia to British businessman Paul Julius de Reuter; facing intense domestic pressure, the shah cancels the pact a year later.

1876: On May 30 the Ottoman Sultan Abdulaziz is deposed; he is replaced by Murad V; two months later, Abdulhamid II becomes sultan and agrees to creation of a constitutional monarchy.

1877: The Russo-Turkish War begins, resulting in the loss of Ottoman territory in the Balkans.

1878: On February 14 Sultan Abdulhamid II closes the Ottoman parliament and suspends the constitution.

1890: Nasser al-Din sells Persian tobacco rights to British interests, sparking countrywide unrest and protests.

1894: Opponents to Sultan Abdulhamid II form the Committee of Union and Progress (CUP); members are known as the Young Turks.

1896: On May 1 Nasser al-Din is assassinated by a follower of a radical anti-Western cleric.

1905: Beginning of Constitutional Revolution in Persia, resulting in establishment of a parliament and adoption of a constitution.

1906: On June 17 Persian troops fire into a crowd of protesters, killing one man and forcing some 20,000 Persians to seek sanctuary on the grounds of the

British embassy; on October 7, the first majlis convenes in Persia.

1907: Great Britain and Russia sign Anglo-Russian Convention, carving up Persia between the two powers.

1908: On June 23 Russian troops enter Tehran and close down the majlis; on July 23 rebels seize control of Macedonia's government, forcing Ottoman Sultan Abdulhamid to share power with a parliament.

1909: On March 31 Islamic leaders stage a coup against the CUP-led government in Istanbul; the CUP soon regroups and ousts the rebels. In July Persian Shah Muhammad Ali abdicates after pro-democracy rebels recapture Tehran.

1911: On December 24 Russian troops close down the Persian majlis on the orders of Shah Ahmad.

1912: On October 8 the First Balkan War erupts as Serbia, Montenegro, Bulgaria, and Greece attack Ottoman troops, seeking to end imperial control over the Balkans.

1913: Second Balkan War is fought by former allies over how to divide Ottoman territories on the peninsula.

1914: The First World War begins in August. Ottoman leaders soon forge an alliance with Germany, while Persia declares neutrality.

1915: Turkish troops defend the Gallipoli Peninsula from an Allied invasion; the Ottoman-sanctioned massacre of Armenians begins.

1916: The Great Arab Revolt challenges Ottoman rule in the Middle East.

1918: The Ottoman Empire agrees to stop fighting on October 30; the Committee of Union and Progress is dissolved and Allied troops occupy Istanbul.

1919: Treaty of Versailles strips Ottoman empire of all territory outside Anatolia.

1921: On February 21 Reza Khan seizes control of Iran in a military coup.

1923: Mustafa Kemal Atutürk becomes the first president of the Republic of Turkey.

1924: On March 3 Turkey's National Assembly exiles Sultan Mehmed VI, ending more than six centuries of Ottoman rule.

1925: On October 31 Shah Ahmad is deposed in Iran, ending more than a century of Qajar rule.

Bolshevik—A Russian political movement that established a communist regime in Russia in 1917.

conscription—duty to serve in the military required under law.

constitutional monarchy—system of government in which a king or other monarch agrees to share power with a parliament and follow laws established by a constitution.

coup d'etat—sudden overthrow of a government and seizure of political power, often involving violence or intervention by the state's military.

fiefdom—society in which all land is owned by the royalty and nobility while all other citizens are forced to tend the land and live in virtual poverty of slavery.

genocide—the deliberate and systematic elimination of an ethnic group, race, or category of people.

Islam—one of the world's major religions, based on the teachings of the Prophet Muhammad. Muslims, as followers of Islam are called, believe that there is only one God, Allah, and that his directions to humans on how to live a good life can be found in the Qur'an.

mahdi—A mystical leader who Muslims believe will lead the transformation of society into a perfect Islamic world.

mosques—places where Muslims worship Allah.

Muslims—followers of the Islamic faith who submit to the will of Allah.

nationalism—a spirit of devotion to one's own country or homeland, often sparking calls for independence.

parliament—a nation's legislative body, typically made up of elected representatives.

prime minister——the leading minister or head of state. Some prime ministers are elected by parliaments, while others are appointed by monarchs.

Qur'an——Islam's holy scriptures, containing Allah's revelations to the Prophet Muhammad.

secular——a society or system of government that is free from religious influences.

Sharia——based on the Qur'an and other sources of Islamic learning, the Sharia sets forth the moral goals of an Islamic society governing a Muslim's religious political, social and private life. Different Islamic societies interpret the Sharia differently, some providing a more liberal interpretation while others interpret the Sharia quite conservatively.

Shia Muslims——members of the second-largest sect within Islam. Shiites revere the descendants of the Prophet Muhammad, and hold other practices and beliefs not shared by members of the largest sect, Sunni Islam. Nearly all Iranians are Shiite Muslims.

Treaty of Versailles——treaty signed in Versailles, France, that ended World War I and established new borders for countries liberated by the war as well as the nations defeated in the conflict.

Bosworth, Edmond, and Carole Hillenbrand, editors. *Qajar Iran: Political, Social and Cultural Changes, 1800–1925.* Costa Mesa, Calif.: Mazda Publishers, 1992.

Busse, Heribert. *History of Persia Under Qajar Rule.* New York: Columbia University Press, 1972.

Durant, Will, and Ariel Durant. *The Age of Napoleon: A History of European Civilization from 1789 to 1815.* New York: Simon and Schuster, 1975.

Finkel, Caroline. *Osman's Dream: The History of the Ottoman Empire.* New York: Basic Books, 2005.

Goodwin, Jason. *Lords of the Horizon: A History of the Ottoman Empire.* New York: Henry Holt and Co., 1998.

Keddie, Nikki R. *Qajar Iran and the Rise of Reza Khan.* Costa Mesa, Calif.: Mazda Publishers, 1999.

Mackey, Sandra. *The Iranians: Persia, Islam and the Soul of a Nation.* New York: Plume, 1998.

Marshall, S.L.A. *The American Heritage History of World War I.* New York: American Heritage Publishing Co., 1982.

Miller, Judith. *God has Ninety-nine Names: Reporting from a Militant Middle East.* New York: Touchstone, 1997.

Palmer, Alan. *The Decline and Fall of the Ottoman Empire.* New York: M. Evans and Co., 1992.

Spencer, William. *Iran: Land of the Peacock Throne.* Tarrytown, N.Y.: Benchmark Books, 1997.

Strachan, Hew. *The First World War.* New York: Viking, 2003.

Wheatcroft, Andrew. *The Ottomans.* London: Viking, 1993.

Zachary, Kent. *World War I: The War to End Wars.* Berkeley Heights, N.J.: Enslow Publishers, 1994.

http://www.qajarpages.org

This Web site provides a history of the Qajar dynasty, reproductions of Qajar portraits, drawings and photographs depicting lifestyles of the Qajar shahs, and essays written by historians analyzing Iran under Qajar rule.

http://www.wsu.edu/~dee/OTTOMAN/CONTENTS.HTM

Comprehensive Web site on the history of the Ottoman empire maintained by Washington State University; the site includes an extensive history of the empire, profiles of major Ottoman sultans, a glossary of terms, and links to other web sites exploring the Ottoman regime.

http://www.crimeanwar.org/

This Web site includes an overview of the war as well as a chronology of events. By using the site's search engine, students can find many articles and essays about the Ottomans as well as other participants in the war.

http://www.pbs.org/greatwar/

Companion Web site to the eight-part PBS documentary The Great War and the Shaping of the 20th Century. The site explores World War I, providing a timeline; analyses of key battles, including Gallipoli; commentaries by historians and an assessment of how the outcome of the war continues to affect international politics nearly a century after the armistice.

Numbers in **bold italic** refer to captions.

Contributors

Hal Marcovitz lives in Chalfont, Pennsylvania, with his wife and daughters, Ashley and Michelle. He is the author of more than 100 books for young readers.

Picture Credits